SPEAK ONLY...
If You Can Improve Upon the Silence

A Book of Quotations on Speaking,
Leadership, and Life

By Maria Hoogterp

Edited by Ellen Kieras
and Jennifer Matteson

ISBN 10: 1-61720-391-6
ISBN 13: 978-1-61720-391-6
First Edition

10 9 8 7 6 5 4 3 2 1

To our parents...

Sally Carungay and Tony Abuan—
and my aunt, Dr. Fely Carungay,

Bill and Judy Hoogterp

for all *your* inspirational quotes, including the ones
we can't get out of *our* heads now that we
are the ones raising kids.

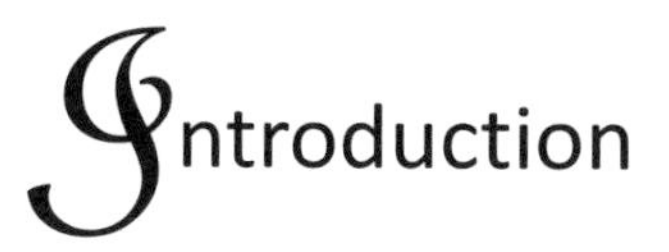

Gifts are not the shiny paper and brilliant bows twinkling in the light but the wonder of what lies hidden in the darkness.

I like to think life's miracles are the same...not apparent to the eye and requiring the soul. If the soul looks at life through a lens, these kinds of quotes help to clean it and make it clearer.

So we are happy to give this small gift of wisdom to you as you lead in making the world a better place, each in your own way. It was especially fun to have our kids' help in making it for you.

So I'll close with something I noticed watching our little ones and others: Children may know less but they love more. At the end of the day, I know what I would choose. Let your inner child out!

Maria

Foreword

These quotes were originally compiled by my wife, Maria, as they were needed for Level 3 of *The Speaking Seminar™* where participants practice voice modulation. She has added to and edited them as the number of trainings has grown. There are always requests after each class for copies, so compiling became a family project. Peter helped pick the fonts and Anna painted the colors.

"Speak Only...If You Can Improve Upon the Silence" was the favorite for a title among class participants and friends. It's the quote that most captured what we were discovering about great speaking, leadership, and life. We'd first heard this quote passed on from Mohandas Gandhi, but a similar version was a saying of the Quakers and other cultures, and a Spanish proverb.

This shows the nature of great sayings. While we've sought to confirm accuracy, we see that wisdom is passed on and rediscovered by each generation in different forms and voices. These are truths not which we invent, but which we recognize and share anew.

Quotations

If your actions inspire others to dream more, learn more,
do more, and become more, you are a leader.
~ John Quincy Adams

Until lions have their historians, tales of the
hunt shall always glorify the hunter.
~ African Proverb

The spirit of the speaker will determine
the spirit of the audience.
~ Roger Ailes

If you want to make God laugh, tell him your plans.
~ Woody Allen

The source of my difficulties has always been
the same: an inability to accept what to others
seems natural and an irresistible tendency to
voice opinions no one wants to hear...
~ Isabel Allende

Enjoy your life, son, 'cause nobody gets out
with a dime and nobody gets out alive.
~ John Amos Sr.

I've learned that people will forget what you have said, people will forget what you did, but people will never forget how you made them feel.
~ Maya Angelou

To live is to choose. But to choose well, you must know who you are and what you stand for; where you want to go and why you want to get there.
~ Kofi Annan

Four things come not back—the spoken word, the sped arrow, the past life, and the neglected opportunity.
~ Arabian Proverb

WE ARE WHAT WE REPEATEDLY DO.

EXCELLENCE, THEREFORE,

IS NOT AN ACT BUT A HABIT.

~ Aristotle

No general can fight his battles alone. He must depend upon his lieutenants and his success depends upon his ability to select the right man for the right place.
~ Philip Armour

Seek first to understand; then to be understood.
~ St. Francis of Assisi

Before you tell me how much you love your God, show me in how much you love all His children. I'm less interested in how you pray or what you say than in how you choose to live and how much love you choose to give.

~ Cory A. Booker

It’s a great relief not to be perfect. Making mistakes is part of the human experience. Admitting to them allows you to learn from them and grow. Others will respect you more for your openness and transparency.

~ Diana Aviv

A wise man will make more opportunities than he finds.

~ Francis Bacon

You don't get to choose how you are going to die or when. You can only decide how you're going to live.

~ Joan Baez

Great leaders ask questions that lead the individual to solve the problem or create the opportunity... hence learning takes place.

~ David Ball

LIFE ALWAYS GIVES US THE TEACHER WE NEED AT EVERY MOMENT.

~ Carlo Joko Beck

Biography is about chaps, but geography is about maps.

~ Edmund Bentley

Making predictions is a very hard thing to do,
especially when it's about the future.
~ Yogi Berra

DREAMS COME A SIZE TOO BIG

SO WE MAY GROW INTO THEM.

~ Josie Bisset

Those who control their passions do so because their
passions are weak enough to be controlled.
~ William Blake

What is conceived well is expressed clearly.
~ Nicolas Boileau

When I give a minister an order, I leave it
to him to find the means to carry it out.
~ Napoleon Bonaparte

We don't think ourselves into a new way of acting,
we act ourselves into a new way of thinking.
~ Larry Bossidy

Most of the things worth doing in the world had been
declared impossible before they were done.
~ Louis D. Brandeis

Ah, but a man's reach should exceed
his grasp, or what's a heaven for?
~ Robert Browning

Enough is a feast.
~ Buddhist Proverb

Success is getting what you want.
Happiness is wanting what you get.
~ Warren Buffett

Make no little plans; they have
no magic to stir men's blood.
~ Daniel H. Burnham

I am a grinder and my favorite quote comes from
Ben Franklin: "Little strokes fell great oaks."
~ Jeb Bush

The privilege of a lifetime is being who you are.
~ Joseph Campbell

You can conquer almost any fear
if you will make up your mind to do so.
For remember, fear doesn't exist anywhere
except in the mind.
~ Dale Carnegie

"There's no use in trying," Alice said.
"One can't believe impossible things."

"I daresay you haven't had much practice,"
said the Queen. "When I was your age, I did it for
a half an hour a day. Why, sometimes I've believed as
many as six impossible things before breakfast."
~ Lewis Carroll

GRASP THE SUBJECT, THE WORDS WILL FOLLOW.
~ Cato The Elder

Focus has nothing to do with limitation...
and everything to do with expansion.
~ Judy Chicago

Not all paths are straight and not all meanings
are apparent. Enjoy your journey.
~ Farai Chideya

When planning for a year, plant corn.
When planning for a decade, plant trees.
When planning for life, train and educate people.
~ Chinese Proverb

You have infinite potential.
Don't compromise yourself by defining yourself.
~ Deepak Chopra

I think that's the way it will work for us all. Don't worry about the level of individual prominence you have achieved; worry about the individuals you have helped become better people. This is my final recommendation: Think about the metric by which your life will be judged and make a resolution to live every day so that in the end your life will be judged a success.
~ Clayton Christensen

**SUCCESS IS NOT FINAL, FAILURE IS NOT FATAL.
IT IS THE COURAGE TO CONTINUE THAT COUNTS.
WE ARE STILL MASTERS OF OUR FATE.
WE ARE STILL CAPTAINS OF OUR SOULS.**
~ Winston Churchill

The only way of finding the limits of the possible is by going beyond them into the impossible.
~ Arthur C. Clarke

It is more important to be loving than right.

~ Ray Chambers

from Lexie Potamkin

Any time you have an opportunity to make
a difference in this world and you don't,
then you are wasting your time on Earth.
~ Roberto Clemente

Mind your wants because somebody wants your mind.
~ George Clinton

If folks can learn to be racist, then they can learn to be
antiracist. If being a sexist ain't genetic then, dad gum,
people can learn about gender equality.
~ Johnetta Cole

Our greatest glory is not in never falling
but in rising every time we fall.
~ Confucius

Fix the problem, not the blame.
~ Sean Connery, *Rising Sun*

As citizens of the world it is imperative that we get
off the back decks of our lives, on to the front porch,
and into the community. Let's join hands to sustain a
climate and culture in which every child can develop into a
healthy, safe, educated, connected, employable,
interdependent, contributing citizen of the world!
~ Ann Cramer

Only after the last tree has been cut down;
Only after the last fish has been caught;
Only after the last river has been poisoned;
Only then will you realize that money cannot be eaten.
~ Cree Indian Prophecy

We must have perseverance and, above all, confidence in ourselves. We must believe that we are gifted for something and that this thing must be attained.
~ Marie Curie

The hottest places in hell are reserved for those who, in times of moral crisis, maintain their neutrality.
~ Dante

OBSTACLES CANNOT CRUSH ME. EVERY OBSTACLE YIELDS TO STERN RESOLVE. HE WHO IS FIXED TO A STAR DOES NOT CHANGE HIS MIND.
~ Leonardo DaVinci

Let us cry for the spilt milk, by all means, if by doing so we learn how to avoid spilling any more. Much wisdom is learnt through tears, but none by forgetting our lessons.
~ Maria Amparo Ruiz De Burton

If you want to build a ship, don't drum up the men to gather wood, divide the work, and give orders. Instead, teach them to yearn for the vast and endless sea.
~Antoine de Saint Exupery

If you don't know what you want to achieve in your presentation, your audience never will.
~ Harvey Diamond

WHETHER I SHALL TURN OUT TO BE THE HERO OF MY OWN LIFE, OR WHETHER THAT STATION WILL BE HELD BY ANYBODY ELSE, THESE PAGES MUST SHOW.
~ Charles Dickens

Let thy speech be better than silence, or be silent.
~ Dionysius of Halicarnassus

The fool wonders.
The wise man asks.
~ Benjamin Disraeli

If there is no struggle, there is no progress.
Those who profess to favor freedom, and yet
depreciate agitation, want crops without plowing
up the ground. They want rain without thunder and
lightning. They want the ocean without the awful roar
of its many waters. Power concedes nothing without a
demand. It never did and it never will.
~ Frederick Douglass

Giving people fish sometimes is needed. Teaching them
to fish is better. However, there is nothing more powerful
than transforming the fishing industry.
~ Bill Drayton

Wherever you find something extraordinary,
you'll find the fingerprints of a great teacher.
~ Arne Duncan

Don't throw away your old shoes
until you have got new ones.
~ Dutch Proverb

IF YOU CHANGE THE WAY YOU LOOK AT THINGS,

THE THINGS YOU LOOK AT CHANGE.

~ Wayne Dyer

Now at last we can begin.
~ Crystal Eatman

The generous and bold
have the best lives.
~ Poetic Edda

Service is the rent we each pay for living.
It is not something to do in your spare time.
It is the very purpose of life.
~ Marian Wright Edelman

OPPORTUNITY IS MISSED BY MOST PEOPLE BECAUSE IT IS DRESSED IN OVERALLS AND LOOKS LIKE WORK. GENIUS IS ONE PERCENT INSPIRATION, NINETY-NINE PERCENT PERSPIRATION. IF WE ALL DID THE THINGS WE ARE CAPABLE OF, WE WOULD ASTOUND OURSELVES.
~ Thomas Edison

Classrooms are dream catchers because
tomorrow's dreams are realized or lost
through today's education.
~ Betty Edwards

Famed interviewer from *Inside the Actors Studio*, James Lipton, was himself interviewed by *Commerce Magazine: The Business of New Jersey.*

Q. What sound or noise do you love?

A. Silence; deep, velvety silence. It is the most underestimated sound on earth, and because of the way we live, we very seldom experience it.

You are a child of the Universe. No less than the trees and the stars you have a right to be here. And whether or not it is clear to you, no doubt the Universe is unfolding as it should.

~ Max Ehrmann

Logic will get you from A to B. Imagination will take you anywhere.

~ Albert Einstein

Leadership: The art of getting someone else to do something you want done because he wants to do it.

~ Dwight D. Eisenhower

He is no fool who gives what he cannot keep to gain that which he cannot lose.

~ Jim Elliot

DO NOT GO WHERE THE PATH MAY LEAD. GO INSTEAD WHERE THERE IS NO PATH AND LEAVE A TRAIL.

~ Ralph Waldo Emerson

Every man's censure is first moulded in his own nature.

~ English Proverb

We never know the worth of water till the well is dry.
~ English Proverb

ಹಿಹಿ

YOU HAVE TWO EARS AND ONE MOUTH.

USE THEM PROPORTIONATELY.

~ Epictetus

ಹಿಹಿ

When spiders unite, they can tie down a lion.
~ Ethiopian Proverb

Do it right, do it once, and do it now.
Ask yourself this question: Who trusts
me and why? You can do something
about the answer. I am still looking
for the "they" after 28 years in the
U.S. Navy...take ownership.
~ Rear Admiral Craig Faller

Furthermore, democracy is, in practice,
merely a tamed civil war.
~ *Financial Times*

The strongest guard is placed at the gateway
to nothing. Maybe because the condition of
emptiness is too shameful to be divulged.
~ F. Scott Fitzgerald

I never told a victim story about my imprisonment.
Instead, I told a transformation story—about how
prison changed my outlook, about how I saw
that communication, truth, and trust are
at the heart of power.
~ Fernando Flores

If there is any one secret of success, it lies in the ability to
get the other person's point of view and see things
from that person's angle as well as from your own.
~ Henry Ford

Tell me and I forget. Teach me and I remember.
Involve me and I learn.
~ Benjamin Franklin

What! No star, and you are going out to sea?
Marching, and you have no music?
Traveling, and you have no book?
What! No love, and you are going out to live?
~ French Proverb

YOU CANNOT TEACH PEOPLE ANYTHING—YOU CAN ONLY HELP THEM DISCOVER IT IN THEMSELVES.
~ Galilei

It’s the action, not the fruit of the action, that's important. You have to do the right thing. It may not be in your power, may not be in your time, that there'll be any fruit. But that doesn't mean you stop doing the right thing. You may never know what results come from your action. But if you do nothing, there will be no result.

~ Mohandas Gandhi

Meaning is not something you stumble across, like the answer to a riddle or the prize in a treasure hunt. Meaning is something you build into your life.

~ John Gardner

As we look ahead into the next century, leaders will be those who empower others.

~ Bill Gates

Inspect what you expect; it helps you catch people doing things right, to applaud them. And often ask yourself, “Towards what end?” It causes me to do or say things and, more importantly, to *not* do or say things.

~ Lucia DiNapoli Gibbons

Behavior dictates privilege.
~ Icema Gibbs

Your living is determined not so much by what life brings to you as by the attitude you bring to life; not so much by what happens to you as by the way your mind looks at what happens.
~ Kahlil Gibran

It's not worth hating because half of those you hate don't know and the other half don't care so the only one you hurt is yourself.
~ Michael Gilfillan

Babies are just plain smarter than we are, at least if being smart means being able to learn something new. They think, draw conclusions, make predictions, look for explanations, and even do experiments.
In fact, scientists are successful precisely because they emulate what children do naturally.
~ Alison Gopnik

There are three things to aim at in public speaking: first, to get into your subject, then to get your subject into yourself and, lastly, to get your subject into the heart of your audience.
~ Alexander Gregg

Michael Moore:
If you were to talk directly to the kids of Columbine, what would you say to them?

Marilyn Manson:
I wouldn't say a single word to them. I would listen to what they have to say.

The only thing that matters in life is health, family, and friends—all the rest is theater!
~ Samuel A. Hardage

Good relationship builders are proactive at decreasing the anxiety and allaying the concerns of others.
~ “Rethinking Trust”
Harvard Business Review

Life is more likely supposed to be a search for people, not for things.
~ Christy Haubegger

The very essence of leadership is that you have to have a vision.
~ Rev. Ted Hesburg

If I am not for myself, who will be for me?
If I am not for others, what am I?
And if not now, when?
~ Rabbi Hillel

There comes a point where we have admired
the problem long enough. Stop admiring
the problem. Do something.
~ Mellody Hobson

**IN TIMES OF CHANGE, THE LEARNERS INHERIT THE EARTH,
WHILE THE LEARNED FIND THEMSELVES BEAUTIFULLY
EQUIPPED TO DEAL WITH A WORLD
THAT NO LONGER EXISTS.**
~ Eric Hoffer

Adversity has the effect of eliciting talents which in
prosperous circumstances would have lain dormant.
~ Homer

If you hire only those you understand, the company
will never get people better than you are.
Always remember that you often find outstanding
people among those you don't particularly like.
~ Soichiro Honda

All it takes is all you got!
~ Judy Hoogterp

YOU CAN EITHER LOOK FOR REASONS TO SUCCEED,

OR FIND EXCUSES TO FAIL.

WHAT ARE YOU SEARCHING FOR?

~ Desmond Howard

No man would listen to you talk if he
didn't know it was his turn next.
~ E.W. Howe

Companies usually don't want to be first.
They would rather pay twice as much to be second.
~ Reginald Hudlin

Fearlessness is like a muscle. I know from my own
life that the more I exercise it the more natural
it becomes to not let my fears run me.
~ Arianna Huffington

To love another person is to see the face of God.
~ Victor Hugo

Every ceiling, when reached, becomes a floor,
upon which one walks as a matter of course
and prescriptive right.
~ Aldous Huxley

In the end, all business operations can be reduced
to three words: people, products, and profits.
Unless you've got a good team,
you can't do much with the other two.
~ Lee Iacocca

Respect the past in the full measure of its deserts,
but do not make the mistake of confusing it with
the present, nor seek in it the ideals of the future.
~ Jose Ingenieros

In order to have friends you must first be one.
~ Jerry Inzerillo

Dance as if no one's watching, sing as if no one's
listening, and live everyday as if it were your last.
~ Irish Proverb

**AT THE END OF THE GAME, THE KING AND
THE PAWN GO BACK IN THE SAME BOX.**
~ Italian Proverb

Most creative work is a process of people passing ideas
and inspirations from the past into the future and
adding their own creativity along the way.
~ Joichi Ito

Time is neutral and does not change things.
With courage and initiative,
leaders change things.
~ Jesse Jackson

My great grandparents would stick a ten-cent piece
in the corner of all correspondence to their children
so that they would always have money
to find their way home. They would sign all
correspondence to their children with this
mid-twentieth century Alabama Gulf Coast
saying: "Remember and be careful every day."
~ Kern Jackson

FALL SEVEN TIMES, GET UP EIGHT.

~ Japanese Proverb

The human brain starts working the moment
you are born and never stops until you
stand up to speak in public.
~ George Jessel

Think 100 times before you take a decision. But once that
decision is taken, stand by it as one man.
~ Muhammed Ali Jinnah

There are two
kinds of people:
those who have been humbled
and those who are about to be.

~ Ethan Penner

Here is to love, the only fire against
which there is no insurance.
~ Dottie Johnson

Always and never are two words you should
always remember never to use.
~ Wendell Johnson

The creative mind plays with the objects it loves.
~ Carl Jung

Celebrate the child-like mind. Play every day.
Embrace lifelong learning. Do something new.
Physical exercise is repetitive;
mental exercise is eclectic.
~ Steve Jurvetson

To be damned by the devil is to be truly blessed.
~ Quai Chang Kane

Most of the clever things
Ben Franklin said, I agree with!
~ Don Karp

You don't get what you deserve,
you get what you negotiate.
~ Dr. Chester Karrass

I AM ONLY ONE, BUT STILL I AM ONE.

I CANNOT DO EVERYTHING,

BUT STILL I CAN DO SOMETHING.

I WILL NOT REFUSE TO DO

THE SOMETHING I CAN DO.

~ Helen Keller

The future does not belong to those who are content with today; pathetic toward common problems and their fellow man and woman alike; timid and fearful in the face of new ideas and bold projects. Rather the future belongs to those who can blend vision, reason, and courage in a personal commitment of ideals and enterprises of American society.

~ Bobby Kennedy

A vision only works with a limit of time.

~ John F. Kennedy

You hire people for what they know.

You fire people for who they are.

~ Vinod Khosla

THE ULTIMATE MEASURE OF A MAN IS NOT WHERE HE STANDS IN MOMENTS OF COMFORT, BUT WHERE HE STANDS AT TIMES OF CHALLENGE AND CONTROVERSY.

~ Martin Luther King, Jr.

When we would get stuck trying to figure out a gag, one of us would usually start singing this silly drone-like ditty we'd heard: “I'm thinkin' too much...I'm thinkin' too much...." It's a helpful phrase to remind yourself sometimes that you can overthink thinkin’.

~ Rick Kirkman

The world needs your inexperience. There's something about the fresh perspective, the naiveté, the limitless energy that comes along with inexperience that enables you to solve problems that many more experienced people have given up on. One reason not to wait to address the world's biggest problems is that they need your attention *before* you accept the status quo, before you are plagued by the knowledge of what is impossible.

~ Wendy Kopp

There's nothing more demoralizing than a
leader who can't clearly articulate why
we're doing what we're doing.
~ James Kouzes and Barry Posner

Life goes fast. Click. You are fifteen.
Click, click. You are fifty-five.
Click. Click. You are gone.
And so are the people who loved and nurtured you.
~ Lee Kravitz

The trouble with talking too fast is you may
say something you haven't thought of yet.
~ Ann Landers

The outrage of hunger amidst plenty will never be solved
by "experts" somewhere. It will only be solved when
people like you and me decide to act.
~ Francis Moore Lappé

HE WHO SEDULOUSLY ATTENDS, POINTEDLY ASKS, CALMLY SPEAKS, COOLLY ANSWERS, AND CEASES WHEN HE HAS NO MORE TO SAY IS IN POSSESSION OF SOME OF THE BEST REQUISITES OF MAN.

~ Johann Casper Lavater

Your only true failure is dwelling on past failures.
~ Michael Lawrence

WE ARE ALL STRONGER THAN WE THINK WE ARE AND ARE MORE FRAGILE THAN WE EVER IMAGINED.
~ Michelle Kydd Lee

If you can't lead them, beat them.
~ Kai Liebert

No man is good enough
to govern another man
without that other's consent.
~ Abraham Lincoln

I do not love the bright sword for its sharpness, nor the arrow for its swiftness, nor the warrior for his glory. I love only that which they defend, the city of the men of Numenor; and I would have her loved for her memory, her ancientry, her beauty, and her present wisdom. Not feared, save as men may fear the dignity of a man, old and wise.
~ Faramir, *The Lord of the Rings*

According to most studies, people's number one fear is public speaking. Number two is death. Death is number two. Does that sound right? This means to the average person, if you go to a funeral, you're better off in the casket than doing the eulogy.

~ Jerry Seinfeld

Everybody has talent; it's just a matter of moving around until you've discovered what it is.

~ George Lucas

IT'S NOT WHAT YOU SAY,

IT'S WHAT PEOPLE HEAR.

~ Frank Luntz

To find what you seek in the road of life, the best proverb of all is that which says: "Leave no stone unturned."

~ Edward Bulwer Lytton

It's the little things citizens do. That's what will make the difference. My little thing is planting trees.

~ Wangari Maathai

I am not am optimist. I am a prisoner of hope... And as we let our own light shine, we unconsciously give other people permission to do the same.

~ Nelson Mandela

Turn your face to the sun and the shadows fall behind you.

~ Maori Proverb

You will either step forward into growth
or you will step back into safety.
~ Abraham Maslow

Charisma is being more concerned about making
others feel good about themselves than you are in
making them feel good about you.
~ John C. Maxwell

Never doubt that a small group of thoughtful,
committed people can change the world.
Indeed, it is the only thing that ever has.
~ Margaret Mead

**TRUST YOURSELF. CREATE THE KIND OF SELF THAT
YOU WILL BE HAPPY TO LIVE WITH ALL YOUR LIFE.
MAKE THE MOST OF YOURSELF BY FANNING THE
TINY, INNER SPARKS OF POSSIBILITY
INTO FLAMES OF ACHIEVEMENT.**
~ Golda Meir

The ultimate responsibility of a leader is to set a standard
of effort and demand all live up to that standard.
~ Urban Meyer

There are three things Yahweh asks of you;
to act justly, love tenderly, and to
walk humbly with your God.
~ Micah

CHARACTER CONSISTS OF WHAT YOU DO ON THE 3RD AND 4TH TRIES.

~ James Michener

The tree of life is kept alive not by tears, but the knowledge that freedom is real and everlasting.
~ Henry Miller

Life is to be lived not at the level of your head, but at the level of your soul.
~ Gabriella Morris

Olympic championship competition is so serious and intense that it affects your entire metabolism. You feel like it's the end of life at that moment and there is no future. I felt as though I was being marched to my own execution!
~ Edwin C. Moses

Look for capable and, very importantly, courageous people who have a curiosity about their world and a generosity of heart. These are the people who should be our leaders.
~ Jim Mustacchia

Lord, help me to want to be
what you want me to be.
~ Most Rev. John J. Myers

In a business like advertising, whose principal asset goes up and down the elevator, talent is not the only thing. It's everything.
~ Miles S. Nadal

THE REAL ART OF CONVERSATION IS NOT ONLY TO SAY THE RIGHT THING AT THE RIGHT PLACE BUT TO LEAVE UNSAID THE WRONG THING AT THE TEMPTING MOMENT.
~ Dorothy Nevill

To live is to change. To be perfect
is to have changed often.
~ Cardinal Newman

If I have seen further than others, it is because
I was standing on the shoulders of giants.
~ Sir Isaac Newton

You are responsible for your own careers, plural.
You need to be curious, to look for opportunities
that interest you, and not be afraid to take risks.
~ Beth Nickels

To do great things is difficult; but to
command great things is more difficult.
~ Friedrich Nietzsche

We don't see things as they are.
We see things as we are.
~ Anaïs Nin

I believe that fortitude is key.
More than anything, be consistent.
Go at it. Go at it. Go at it.
~ Antonia Novello

BE THE PERSON YOU ADMIRE.

~ Ron Olson

Our deepest fear is not that we are inadequate. Our deepest fear is that we are powerful beyond measure. It is our light, not our darkness that most frightens us. We ask ourselves, “Who am I to be brilliant, gorgeous, talented, fabulous?” Actually, who are you not to be? You are a child of God. Your playing small does not serve the world. There is nothing enlightened about shrinking so that other people won’t feel insecure around you. We are all meant to shine, as children do. We were born to make manifest the glory of God that is within us. It's not just in some of us; It’s in everyone.

~ Marianne Williamson

How old would you be if you
didn't know how old you were?
~ Satchel Paige

The arc of the moral universe is long,
but it bends toward justice.
~ Theodore Parker

FIND OUT WHO YOU ARE AND DO IT ON PURPOSE.

~ Dolly Parton

Never tell people how to do things. Tell them what to do and they will surprise you with their ingenuity.
~ George Patton

The bigger the problem, the bigger the opportunity.
~ Luigi Tiziano Peccenini

To be good is expected. To be better is the challenge.
~ Christi Pedra

We judge ourselves by our intentions.
Others judge us by our actions.
~ Ian Percy

Speak when you are angry—and you will
make the best speech you'll ever regret.
~ Laurence J. Peter

Each second we live is a new and unique moment of the universe, a moment that will never be again. And what do we teach our children? We teach them that two and two make four and that Paris is the capital of France. When will we also teach them what they are? We should say to each of them: "Do you know what you are? You are a marvel. You are unique. In all the years that have passed, there has never been another child like you."
~ Pablo Picasso

The harder you work, the luckier you get.
~ Gary Player

LIVING CONSCIOUSLY INVOLVES BEING GENUINE. IT INVOLVES LISTENING AND RESPONDING TO OTHERS HONESTLY AND OPENLY. IT INVOLVES BEING IN THE MOMENT.
~ Sidney Poitier

One of the great wisdoms among start-ups is
“knowing what you don't know is much
more valuable than what you know.”
~ Kim Polese

Rely on your own strength of body and soul.
Fire above the mark you intend to hit.
Energy and invincible determination with the
right motive are the levers that move the world.
~ Noah Porter

Perseverance and practice will always outlast talent.
~ Nick Price

The real voyage of discovery consists not in seeing
new landscapes but in having new eyes.
~ Marcel Proust

My favorite quote, by William H. Johnsen, captures ten of
the most powerful words in the English language, each
only two letters. “If it is to be, it is up to me!”
~ Bob Provost

The thing that is really hard, and really
amazing, is giving up on being perfect and
beginning the work of becoming yourself.
~ Anna Quindlen

COURAGE DOES NOT ALWAYS ROAR.
SOMETIMES COURAGE IS THE QUIET VOICE AT THE END OF THE DAY SAYING, "I WILL TRY AGAIN TOMORROW."

~ Mary Anne Radmacher

Early movers may convince themselves they are geniuses, even though they are only the leaders of a herd that is rapidly headed toward a cliff.

~ Raghuram G. Rajan

Whatever the heart loves, the head must think about; what the head thinks about, the mouth must speak of; whatever the mouth speaks of the hand must do.

~ Monsignor Gregory Ramkissoon

Always be shorter than anybody dared to hope.

~ Lord Reading

Everything you need to be successful in business or life, you learned in kindergarten: listen, learn, and be nice to others. Oh, and raise your hand if you have to go potty...that one's important too.

~ Joseph A.M. Ricci

True eloquence consists in saying all that
should be said, and that only.
~ La Rochefoucauld

It is better to live one day as a lion
than a thousand days as a lamb.
~ Roman Proverb

**PEOPLE GROW THROUGH EXPERIENCE,
IF THEY MEET LIFE HONESTLY AND COURAGEOUSLY.
THIS IS HOW CHARACTER IS BUILT.
DO WHAT YOU CAN, WITH WHAT YOU HAVE,
WHERE YOU ARE.**
~ Eleanor Roosevelt

Be sincere. Be brief. Be seated.
~ Franklin D. Roosevelt

Far better it is to dare mighty things, to win
glorious triumphs, even though checkered by
failure, than to take rank with those poor
spirits who neither enjoy much nor suffer
much, because they live in the gray twilight
that knows not victory nor defeat.
~ Theodore Roosevelt

It is what you read when you don't have to that determines what you will be when you can't help it.

~ Oscar Wilde

IT'S NOT HOW STRONGLY YOU FEEL ABOUT YOUR TOPIC, IT'S HOW STRONGLY THEY FEEL ABOUT YOUR TOPIC AFTER YOU SPEAK.

~ Tim Salladay

Water that does not move is always shallow.
~ Sami Proverb

There is nothing human beings do that
they can't get better at if they practice.
~ Michael Sanchez

Dare to be great.
~ Jon Sandelman

He who allows his day to pass by without
practicing generosity and enjoying life's
pleasures is like a blacksmith's bellows,
he breathes but does not live.
~ Sanskrit Proverb

Make sure you have finished speaking before
your audience has finished listening.
~ Dorothy Sarnoff

My favorite quote was said to me by a guy
I used to know in the street in New York:
He said, "Don't let nobody stop you.
Not nobody. Not never."
~Richard Schiff

If I get visions, I'll visit a doctor.
~ Helmut Schmidt

I have yet to find the man who did not do better work and put forth greater effort under a spirit of approval than under a spirit of criticism.
~ Charles Schwab

LIFE IS A SERIES OF COMEBACKS.

~ Tom Scott

Our plans miscarry because they have no aim. When a man does not know what harbor he is making for, no wind is the right wind.
~ Seneca

Managers manage people.
Leaders manage the system.
~ Peter Senghe

Be humble for you are made of earth.
Be noble for you are made of stars.
~ Serbian Proverb

Don't cry because it's over. Smile because it happened.
~ Dr. Seuss

The reasonable man adapts himself to the world.
The unreasonable one persists in trying to adapt the world to himself. Therefore, all progress depends upon the unreasonable man.
~ George Bernard Shaw

There is amazing influence and moving power gained from people who are inspiring—that moment when someone moves you and your attention is completely absorbed.
~ Wendy Shepherd

The primary role of voluntary associations in American life is to continually shape and reshape
the vision of a more just social order, to propose programs which might lead to the manifestation of that vision, to argue for them with other contenders in the public arena, and to press for adoption and implementation. For voluntary associations to do less than that is to abdicate their civic responsibility.
~ Paul Sherry

People say you should write a book before you die,
but the pages and stories are already written
by those you've touched.
~ William Shue

Much speech is one thing; well-timed speech is another.
~ Sophocles

FOR A LONG TIME IT HAD SEEMED THAT LIFE WAS ABOUT TO BEGIN—REAL LIFE. BUT THERE WERE ALWAYS SOME OBSTACLES IN THE WAY, SOMETHING TO BE GOTTEN THROUGH FIRST, SOME UNFINISHED BUSINESS, TIME STILL TO BE SERVED, A DEBT TO BE PAID. THEN LIFE WOULD BEGIN. AT LAST IT DAWNED ON ME THAT THESE OBSTACLES WERE MY LIFE.
~ Alfred D. Souza

Whoever gossips to you will gossip about you.
~ Spanish Proverb

It's the little things...just be nice...because nice matters.
~ Sarah Steele

Transparency drives commitment.
~ Ullrich Suessbrich

Ultimate excellence lies not in winning every battle
but in defeating the enemy without ever fighting.
~ from Master Sun's *The Art of War*

THERE IS NOTHING I CAN SAY IN MY OWN WORDS THAT COULD IMPROVE ON THE SILENCE WHICH THIS PAINED WORLD SO SORELY NEEDS. I AM AN EDITOR, NOT A CREATOR; A REPEATER, NOT AN ORIGINATOR; A CONGREGANT, NOT A PREACHER.
~ Jeffrey Swartz

Fear less, hope more.
Whine less, breathe more.
Talk less, say more.
Hate less, love more.
And all good things are yours.
~ Swedish Proverb

Anyone can hold the helm when the sea is calm.
~ Publilius Syrus

Getting the players is easy. Getting them to play together is the hard part.

~ Casey Stengel

One who saves but one life, it is as
if they have saved the universe.
~ The Talmud

Knowing requires intelligence;
doing requires courage.
~ Todor Tashev

Someday after mastering the winds, the waves, the tides, and gravity, we shall harness for God the energies of love. And then, for the second time in the history of the world, man will have discovered fire.
~ Pierre Teilhard De Chardin

SEE HOW NATURE—TREES, FLOWERS, GRASS—GROWS IN SILENCE; SEE THE STARS, THE MOON, AND THE SUN, HOW THEY MOVE IN SILENCE... WE NEED SILENCE TO BE ABLE TO TOUCH SOULS.
~ Mother Teresa

You may have to fight a battle
more than once to win it.
~ Margaret Thatcher

In the long run, men hit only what they aim at.
Therefore, they had better aim at something high.
~ Henry David Thoreau

A good word is an easy obligation,
but not to speak ill requires only our silence,
which costs us nothing.
~ John Tillotson

Successful people make decisions quickly
and change them slowly, whereas average
people make decisions slowly, if at all,
and change them quickly.
~ Brian Tracy

Every great dream begins with a dreamer.
Always remember, you have within you the
strength, the patience, and the passion to
reach for the stars to change the world.
~ Harriet Tubman

Well-timed silence hath more eloquence than speech.
~ Martin Farquhar Tupper

The right word may be effective,
but no word was ever as effective
as a rightly timed pause.
~ Mark Twain

Go to the people. Learn from them. Live with them. Start with what they know. Build with what they have. The best of leaders, when the job is done, when the task is accomplished, the people will say we have done it ourselves.

~ Lao Tzu

Opportunities multiply as they are seized.

~ Sun Tzu

If you want to destroy a people, take away their language and their culture will soon disappear.

~ Sabine Ulibarri

THE SKEPTIC DOES NOT MEAN HE WHO DOUBTS, BUT HE WHO INVESTIGATES OR RESEARCHES, AS OPPOSED TO HE WHO ASSERTS AND THINKS THAT HE HAS FOUND.

~ Miguel de Unamuno

Dream big dreams, then put on your overalls!

~ Fred Van Amburgh

Do not let the perfect be the enemy of the good.

~ (take on quote by) Voltaire

Knowing is not enough; we must apply.
Willing is not enough; we must do.
Magic is believing in yourself.
If you can do that,
you can make anything happen.
~ Johann Wolfgang von Goethe

Without inspiration, the best powers of the mind
remain dormant. There is a fuel in us
which needs to be ignited with sparks.
~ Johann Gottfried Von Herder

For today's gain I won't sell the future.
~ Werner von Siemens

The capital T—Truth—is about life before death. It is
about simple awareness—awareness of what is so real
and essential, so hidden in plain sight all around us, that
we have to keep reminding ourselves over and over:
"This is water, this is water."
~ David Foster Wallace

The success of your presentation will be
judged not by the knowledge you send
but by what the listener receives.
~ Lilly Walters

As long as you have nothing to shoot for,
you will always have plenty of ammunition.
~ John Ward

In all things that are purely social, we can be as separate as the fingers, yet one as the hand in all things essential to mutual progress.
~ Booker T. Washington

Be courteous to all, but intimate with few
and let those be well-tried before
you give them your confidence.
~ George Washington

The fastest road to success is
to double the failure rate.
~ Tom Watson

I've learned that mistakes can often
be as good a teacher as success.
~ Jack Welch

Always hire the person,
not just the skill set.
~ Allison Werder

DO ALL THE GOOD YOU CAN,

BY ALL THE MEANS YOU CAN,

IN ALL THE WAYS YOU CAN,

IN ALL THE PLACES YOU CAN,

AT ALL THE TIMES YOU CAN,

TO ALL THE PEOPLE YOU CAN,

AS LONG AS YOU EVER CAN.

~ John Wesley

When choosing between two evils,
I always like to try the one I haven't tried before.

~ Mae West

Seek the lofty by reading, hearing, and seeing great work
at some moment every day.

~ Thornton Wilder

Distance lends enchantment.

~ Paul Wilmot

Leadership does not always wear
the harness of compromise.

~ Woodrow Wilson

Peace of mind is worth a million dollars and,
if you have a million dollars, then it's priceless.
~ Andrea Wishom

If Socrates was right—
"Follow the question where it leads"—
then choose well the questions
you want to pursue.
~ Harris Wofford

The true test of a man's character is
what he does when no one is watching.
Be more concerned with your character
than your reputation, because your character is
what you really are, while your reputation
is merely what others think you are.
The main ingredient of stardom
is the rest of the team.
~ John Wooden

It is never too late to matter.
~ Elaine Wynn

No choice is a choice too.
~ Yiddish Proverb

YOU CAN GET EVERYTHING YOU WANT
IF YOU JUST HELP ENOUGH OTHER PEOPLE
GET WHAT THEY WANT.
~ Zig Ziglar

If you can walk, you can dance.
If you can talk, you can sing.
~ Zimbabwe saying

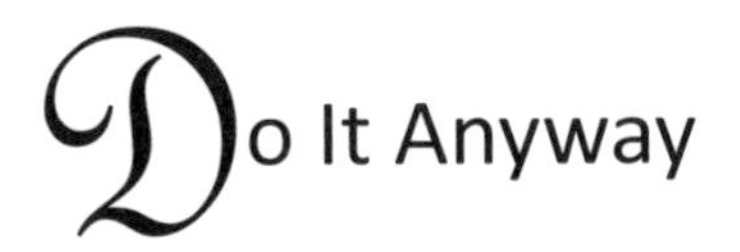

Do It Anyway

People are often unreasonable,
illogical, and self-centered.
Forgive them anyway.
If you are kind, people may accuse you
of selfish ulterior motives.
Be kind anyway.
If you are successful, you will win some
false friends and some true enemies.
Succeed anyway.
If you are honest and frank,
people may cheat you.
Be honest and frank anyway.
What you spend years building,
someone could destroy overnight.
Build anyway.
If you find serenity and happiness,
they may be jealous.
Be happy anyway.
The good you do today,
people will often forget tomorrow.
Do good anyway.
Give the world the best you have,
and it may never be enough.
Give the best you've got anyway.
You see, in the final analysis
it is between you and God;
it was never between you and them anyway.

~ Mother Teresa

We are so grateful to the people who took time out of their busy schedules to share a quote, either their own or one that had meaning for them.

Tom Alexander
Dave Allan
John Amos
Diana Aviv
Michael Balaoing
David Ball
Emma Banks
Celia Bobrowsky
Koen Bogers
Cory A. Booker
Michéle D. Bowman
Steven K. Brisgel
Sylvia Matthews Burwell
Dave Burwick
Jeb Bush
Penny Carolin
Ray Chambers
Farai Chideya
Deepak Chopra
Shakim Compere
Ann Cramer
Julie Fisher Cummings
Chris Dinkel
Bill Drayton
Arne Duncan
Wayne Dyer
Betty Edwards
Maria Eitel
Jan Eliot
Jim Elliot
Sara Erstad
Greg Evans
Craig Faller
Allan Fisher
Jim Fitzgerald
Kelly Flynn
Stephen Friedman
Ann Fudge
Piersten Gaines
Lucia DiNapoli Gibbons
Icema Gibbs
Michael Gilfillan
Evie Goldfine
Alison Gopnik
Robert Hackett
Beverly Hall
Samuel A. Hardage
Christy Haubegger
Mellody Hobson
Paul Hoogterp
Beverly Horowitz
Desmond Howard
Reginald Hudlin
Arianna Huffington
Jerry Inzerillo
Kern Jackson
Javier Jaime
Dottie Johnson
Steve Jurvetson
Don Karp
Sheila Kelley
Rick Kirkman
Wendy Kopp
Martha Kramer
Lee Kravitz
Michael Lawrence
Michelle Kydd Lee
Kate Lewis
Yun Chi Li
Kai Liebert
Rick Little
Li Lu
Josh Lucas
Frank Luntz
Edward Gerhard Martin
Joseph Mayock
Rita F. Menz
Urban Meyer
Brigitte Mohn
Gabriella Morris
Edwin C. Moses
Jim Mustacchia
Most Rev. John J. Myers
Miles S. Nadal
Beth Nickels

Soledad O'Brien
Jane Olson
Ron Olson
Reimar Paschke
David Paull
Kathy Havens Payne
Luigi Tiziano Peccenini
Christi Pedra
Ethan Penner
Angelika Peters
Kim Polese
Roberto Pradilla
Nick Price
Bob Provost
German Ramirez
Msgr Gregory Ramkissoon
Joseph A.M. Ricci
David H. Rice
Mickie Rinehart
Jennifer Hoos Rothberg
Jason Rzepka
Gregory Sachs
Michael Sanchez
Jon Sandelman
Christine Scheffler
Richard Schiff
Jacob Schimmel
Jeff Schwartz
Jeff Swartz
Tom Scott
Steve Seabolt
Wendy Shepherd
Andrew Shue
Elisabeth Shue
Tom Silverman
Silda Wall Spitzer
Anne Steele
Ullrich Suessbrich
Michael Tarino
Todor Tashev
Rhea Turteltaub
Peter Vincent
Rhonda Walton
Paula Weiner
Dolly Wen
Allison Werder
Keith A. Wilmot
Bernard Winograd
Andrea Wishom
Harris Wofford
Jenny Wolpert
Achim Wolter
Allison Wright
Elaine Wynn
Steve Zales

Also, thanks to Arrington Chambliss, Wayne Meisel, Maura Wolf, and Julia Scatliff for letting us be part of the quote book *Light One Candle*, lo those many years ago, which helped inspire this one.

Special thanks to Jim Mustacchia, one of the coolest people we know, for introducing and supporting our work and that of so many others, helping others grow.

Book layout and design
by Jennifer Matteson
Back cover design art
by Ethan Hoogterp

Feedback and input:

As everyone in *The Speaking Seminar™* knows, we *demand* feedback. In the foreword, we recognized that some quotes have evolved from various speakers in history without all of us being able to know clearly who said which first. Even so, efforts were made to ensure accuracy and attribution of quotes and all input is welcome if corrections need to be made.

Have a quote to contribute?

If you would like to submit a quote for consideration and use in *The Speaking Seminar™* classes, go to www.blueplanet.org and click on "Quotes."
We will also welcome jokes (clean ones, please!)
and stories for use in practice during classes.

To order additional copies: www.blueplanet.org

Blue Planet Training is a U.S. based company and LLC. Blue Planet trains executives around the world in communication, public speaking and leadership, primarily through *The Speaking Seminar™*. We also offer leadership courses designed and customized to company specifications and executive coaching to unlock potential to speak and lead.
www.blueplanet.org

The Speaking Seminar™ is the signature training of Blue Planet. It helps leaders in business and all walks of life rapidly improve their ability to communicate to others. Whether public speaking to a large audience, making a comment in a meeting, or talking with someone one on one, most people can be much better.
www.blueplanettraining.com

Each level is one hour, building on the last, to strengthen your ability to be more memorable with less words. Every few minutes is a different exercise, activity, recording of you on camera or game, that has you learning, laughing, and achieving professional skills quickly. When you see on someone's résumé or profile *The Speaking Seminar™* logo, with a number circled, that means they have achieved that level of certification.